FEDERAL BUREAU OF INVESTIGATION

AGENTS OF GOVERNMENT

TERESA WIMMER

Creative Education • Creative Paperbacks

Published by Creative Education and Creative Paperbacks

P.O. Box 227, Mankato, Minnesota 56002
Creative Education and Creative Paperbacks are
imprints of The Creative Company
www.thecreativecompany.us

Design and production by Chelsey Luther
Art direction by Rita Marshall

Printed in Malaysia

Photographs by Alamy (CJG – Technology, Everett Collection Inc.), Corbis (Bettmann, David
Brabyn, David Bro/ZUMA Press, Corbis, Astakhov Dmitry/ITAR-TASS, Hulton-Deutsch
Collection, Ben Margot/AP, Charles Smith, John Swart/AP), deviantART (AllydNYC), Getty
Images (AFP/Stringer, American Stock Archive, Bloomberg, Keystone/Stringer, New York
Daily News Archive, Stegerphoto, Larry Zumwalt/Stringer), Newscom (akg-images, Everett
Collection), Shutterstock (Carlos Caetano, Carolina K. Smith MD, Vacclav)

Library of Congress Cataloging-in-Publication Data
Wimmer, Teresa.
Federal Bureau of Investigation / Teresa Wimmer.
p. cm. — (Agents of government)
Summary: An in-depth look at the people and policies behind the government agency known
as the FBI, from its founding in 1908 to the controversies and challenges it faces today.
Includes bibliographical references and index.

ISBN 978-1-60818-545-0 (hardcover)
ISBN 978-1-62832-146-3 (pbk)
1. United States. Federal Bureau of Investigation. 2. Criminal investigation—United States.
I. Title.

HV8144.F43W56 2015
363.250973—dc23   2014029605

CCSS: RI.5.1, 2, 3, 5, 6, 8; RH.6-8.3, 4, 5, 8

First Edition HC 9 8 7 6 5 4 3 2 1
First Edition PBK 9 8 7 6 5 4 3 2 1

TABLE OF CONTENTS

CHAPTERS

Introduction 4

Law and Disorder 7

Gangs and Controversies 17

Stabilizing Structure 27

Securing the Unknown 37

AGENCY INSIDERS

Emma Goldman 12

Julius and Ethel Rosenberg 22

The Director 32

Tylenol Panic 42

AROUND THE WORLD

Brink's Robbery 15

Public Enemy No. 1 25

The KGB 35

OKBOMB 45

•

Glossary 46

Selected Bibliography 47

Websites 47

Index 48

Before 1908, when the agency that would become known as the Federal Bureau of Investigation (FBI) was created, law enforcement in

the United States was not as organized, powerful, or effective as it is today. Most criminals were brought to justice by state or local governments. Police officers were too often **corrupt** and bribed by politicians to "look the other way." Many police officers, and even some government officials, were hired based more on the politicians they knew than on their skill level. When president Theodore Roosevelt created the agency, he envisioned it as an organization that would help rein in political corruption while enforcing U.S. laws. In 2014, the primary function of the FBI changed from law enforcement to national security to reflect changing priorities in a post-terrorist world. Although the FBI's actions and methods sometimes came under scrutiny, the Bureau remained true to its mission to protect and defend the U.S. against intelligence threats, to uphold and enforce the nation's criminal laws, and to provide leadership and criminal justice services to federal, state, and international agencies. In a sometimes fearful world, the FBI provides Americans with a sense of safety and security.

Theodore Roosevelt's time as police commissioner of New York City informed his later presidential actions.

Law and Disorder

In the mid-1800s, the U.S. was growing rapidly. In search of a fresh start and new fortunes, settlers moved from the East Coast through the West to buy land cheaply and establish farms and ranches. Many criminals took advantage of places governed by a lone, overworked sheriff. Uneasy settlers began to demand more law and order.

To lend national support to the efforts to curb crime, the Department of Justice (DOJ) was created in 1870. Because there was no national police force yet, the DOJ hired private detectives and investigators from other agencies to examine federal crimes. (Such crimes were defined as illegal activities that took place on lands owned by the federal government or that crossed state lines.) However, detectives were often expensive and difficult to find.

Because the U.S. government was designed specifically to share power among many parts, 19th-century Americans feared giving too much power to any one branch. From the country's earliest days, people expected the federal government to oversee matters that affected the nation as a whole but to steer clear of happenings

In the 1880s, groups of settlers traveled together in wagon trains as they crossed the plains of the American West.

within a state. However, by the late 1800s, easier methods of transportation and communication gave people a more positive sense of the government's presence in their lives.

The Industrial Revolution—a period that affected the U.S. in the 1800s and in which many machines were invented for use in factories, manufacturing, farming, and transportation—prompted urban growth. Americans were on the move as never before, and the country's population exploded with a wave of European immigrants seeking freedom and a better life in the New World. As so many different people came together in crowded cities, crime spiked. Many Americans realized a federal law enforcement agency might be able to control certain areas more effectively if it had the right to supervise state and local agencies. The idea of a more powerful federal government, along with an idealistic, reformist spirit, characterized a period known as the Progressive Era (1890s–1920).

Theodore Roosevelt was a leader among Progressives and in reforming law enforcement practices. At the start of his second term as president, in 1905, he appointed fellow Progres-

As so many different people came together in crowded cities, crime spiked.

sive Charles Bonaparte as attorney general. Both men wanted to fight corruption as effectively as possible, but the DOJ under Bonaparte was ill-equipped to do so. It hired agents from the Secret Service to take on one case at a time. And these agents answered to the Secret Service chief, not the DOJ—or Bonaparte. A frustrated Bonaparte appealed to Congress for help. On May 27, 1908, Congress passed a law that blocked the DOJ from hiring Secret Service agents in the future.

The next step was to create a force wholly under the DOJ's control. President Roosevelt, in an effort to end a series of illegal land sales in the West, authorized Bonaparte to hire a few detectives to investigate the matter. In June 1908, the first 34 agents in the new federal law enforcement agency were signed on. This nameless agency had no officially designated leader other than the attorney general until July 26, 1908. At that time, Bonaparte ordered the agents to report to chief examiner Stanley W. Finch.

The force of 34 agents remained part of the DOJ, even after Bonaparte and Roosevelt left office in 1909. The new attorney general, George Wickersham, came up with the name Bureau of

The densely populated working-class neighborhood of Manhattan's Lower East Side typified early 1900s New York.

Families of those imprisoned by the Espionage and Sedition Acts exercised their own rights to speak out in protest.

Investigation (BOI) on March 16, 1909. The title of chief examiner was then changed to "chief."

Because few crimes were classified as federal at the time, the BOI spent its early years investigating matters relating primarily to banking, bankruptcy, land fraud, postal crimes, and violations of federal **antitrust** laws. From the beginning, the public's persistent fears of a federal police force led Congress to ban BOI agents from carrying weapons or making arrests. When the world went to war in 1914—and the U.S. joined in 1917—new fears emerged about immigrants and potential foreign spies. The BOI soon began keeping a close eye on immigrant populations. To help strengthen the BOI's capabilities, Congress increased the BOI's budget by more than $2 million between 1911 and 1920. Its number of agents skyrocketed from 34 in 1908 to 650 in 1924. The agency received help from a legal standpoint, too: The 1917 Espionage Act made it a federal crime to steal government secrets. Then the 1918 Immigration Act allowed the federal government to **deport** legal U.S. immigrants on the grounds of their member-

ship in revolutionary organizations such as the **Communist** Party. BOI investigations led to more than 2,000 arrests and more than 1,000 convictions under the Espionage Act by 1930.

During World War I, the BOI focused its attention on **radical** activists and members of **socialist** and communist parties in America. To aid in the information gathering, the General Intelligence Division (GID) was established as part of the DOJ in 1919 and assigned to the BOI in 1921. Recent laws also discouraged people from getting in the government's way. When the U.S. entered World War I in 1917, Congress made it a criminal act to oppose its wartime decisions. The Sedition Act of 1918 penalized people for speaking out against the U.S. government or promoting the cause of America's enemies. During this period, known as America's first Red Scare, the federal government targeted anyone—especially radicals and immigrants—whom it perceived as being threats to its causes.

The Russian Revolution of 1917 had struck fear in the hearts of Americans who were already alarmed by the rapidly changing times and

BOI investigations led to more than 2,000 arrests and more than 1,000 convictions under the Espionage Act by 1930.

politics of communism. In 1919, 4 million U.S. **union** workers participated in 3,600 nationwide labor strikes to protest low wages and unsafe working conditions. Fearing these strikes would lead to a violent revolution against the federal government, the GID, led by J. Edgar Hoover, raided the meeting places and offices of Communist Labor parties in 30 cities on January 2, 1920. These actions came to be known as the Palmer Raids (after Hoover's boss, attorney general A. Mitchell Palmer) and led to 6,000 arrests and 500 deportations. At first, the Palmer Raids received positive publicity from the mainstream media, but soon people grew disturbed by the GID's broad targeting methods, disregard for search warrants, and questionable interrogation tactics. The raids tarnished the DOJ's and BOI's images in the eyes of Americans. It would take J. Edgar Hoover to make them regain their belief in federal justice methods.

John (known as J.) Edgar Hoover was born in Washington, D.C., on January 1, 1895, and graduated from George Washington University Law School in 1916. He began working for the DOJ in 1917 and rose quickly through the ranks. He became assistant to the attorney general in 1918 and head of the GID in 1919. When the GID joined the Bureau of Investigation in 1921, the

AGENCY INSIDER

EMMA GOLDMAN

One of the most famous **anarchists** and antiwar activists in American history, Emma Goldman was born in Russia in 1869 and emigrated to the U.S. in 1885. She did not believe in the government's right to make war and used her magazine, *Mother Earth*, to promote U.S. military opposition. The BOI arrested her in June 1917, and she was imprisoned for conspiring against the draft. Initially released in 1919, she was re-arrested by Hoover and deported with 248 other foreign-born people labeled as radicals.

Boston's police force joined the 1919 wave of strikes as American laborers tried to gain more control over working conditions.

26-year-old Hoover became assistant director of the BOI. Three years later, he was named director, a title he would hold for the next 48 years.

To repair the BOI's image, Hoover fired several agents whom he considered unqualified and ordered background checks to be conducted for new agent applicants. Along with a special BOI training school in New York, Hoover established an Identification Division within the BOI in July 1924. This division consolidated fingerprint records from the BOI's file with those from state and local police throughout the country.

The centralized database proved invaluable to everyone because it enabled law enforcement to link criminal acts in various locations. Hoover also created the Criminology Laboratory, now known as the FBI Lab, in 1932 as he worked to professionalize investigations by collecting and analyzing physical evidence with the most advanced equipment available. Although some of Hoover's methods would prove to be controversial, he succeeded in making the Bureau an integral part of the national government.

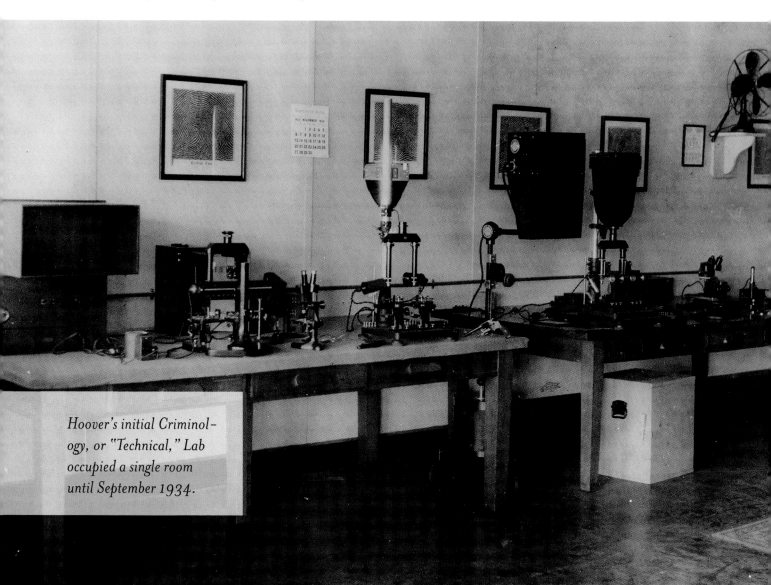

Hoover's initial Criminology, or "Technical," Lab occupied a single room until September 1934.

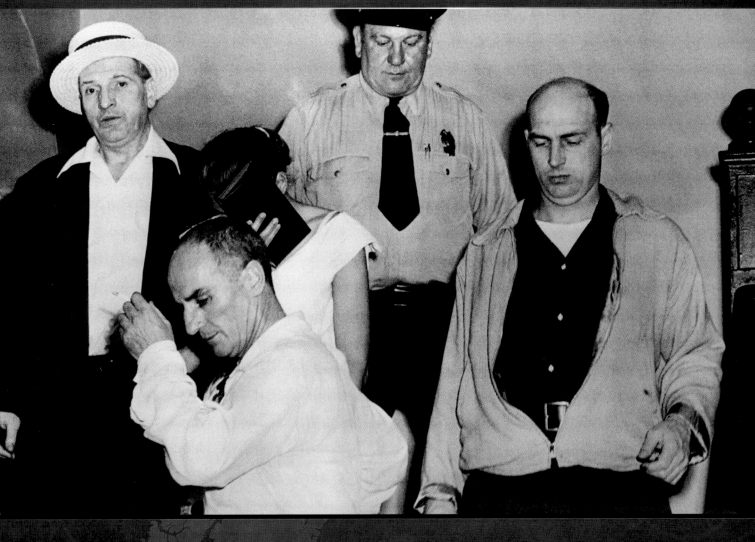

BRINK'S ROBBERY
Boston, Massachusetts, U.S.A.

On January 17, 1950, 11 costumed men broke into the Brink's Building in Boston, Massachusetts, and stole $2.7 million. The culprits were not caught until January 1956, just days before the statute of limitations expired. Joseph "Specs" O'Keefe (above, front) made a deal with the FBI to testify against his conspirators, and eight of them were sentenced to life in prison. Two more died before they could go to trial. A portion of the money was recovered; the rest remains a mystery.

Gangs and Controversies

By the 1930s, the Bureau's image had been repaired, but it still had limited authority and a small budget to enforce laws. However, several things during the 1930s paved the way for a more powerful agency to emerge. After the **stock market** crashed in 1929, a widespread helplessness gripped the country. By 1932, 25 percent of Americans were unemployed. Chaos reigned as banks, businesses, and insurance companies failed. **Gangsters** such as Charles "Pretty Boy" Floyd, John Dillinger, and Bonnie and Clyde traversed the country robbing banks and shooting anyone who tried to stop them. Not even federal law enforcement could catch them. Fearful Americans began to demand more protection.

A string of ransom kidnappings during the 1930s added to the public's safety concerns. Perhaps the most infamous kidnapping occurred on March 1, 1932, when news broke that 20-month-old Charles Lindbergh Jr., son of famous aviator Charles Lindbergh and his wife Anne Morrow Lindbergh, had been taken from his home. Even though kidnapping was not yet considered a federal crime, the BOI was called in to assist

Evidence used against alleged kidnapper Bruno Hauptmann included a ladder made from boards in his attic.

state and local police with the investigation. When the boy's body was found two months later, public outcry demanded a change to the federal law. (The 1948 Federal Kidnapping Act would allow the FBI to be directly involved in kidnappings that crossed state lines.) After an investigation that lasted more than two years, the BOI charged German-born carpenter Bruno Richard Hauptmann with the crime. In a 1935 trial, Hauptmann was found guilty of first-degree murder and sentenced to death.

The trial publicized the BOI's scientific expertise and professionalism during the investigation—including analyzing the handwriting of the ransom notes and hiring experts to scientifically dissect the wooden ladder that was used to reach the boy's room. This greatly enhanced the Bureau's (now known as the FBI) reputation. To aid in their fight against crime, FBI agents were allowed to carry guns and make arrests in the mid-1930s. Funding was also increased. In 1940, the FBI gained sole control to investigate all espionage cases within the U.S. and to monitor the activities of groups considered threats to national defense. However, the FBI remained under the overall authority of the DOJ. Because ongoing FBI investigations were no longer controlled directly by the federal government, accusations arose that Hoover and his agents conducted secret operations—rumors that persisted for the next several decades.

With America's entry into World War II in December 1941, fears about foreign spies in the U.S. prompted Congress to give the FBI even more funds and authority to conduct investigations. Earlier that year, the FBI had broken up the Duquesne Spy Ring in the largest espionage case in U.S. history to end in convictions. The ring, headed by South African–born Frederick "Fritz" Joubert Duquesne, collected government secrets for Germany's Nazi Party. German American William Sebold worked as a double agent to help the FBI bring down the spy ring. All 33 members were arrested and convicted before they could carry out their goals.

During and after World War II, Western governments were concerned that communism would spread from the Soviet Union to other countries. By 1945, the Bureau had become completely refocused on such counterintelligence measures as wiretapping, bug planting,

In 1940, the FBI gained sole control to investigate all espionage cases within the U.S.

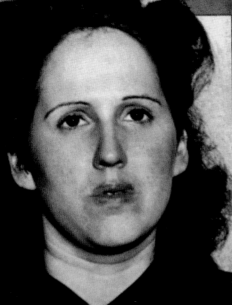
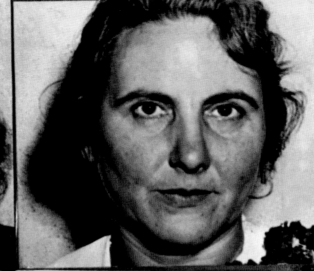

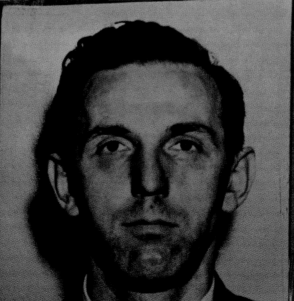
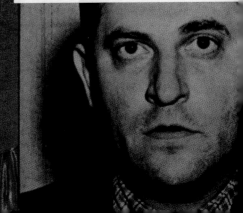

The FBI secretly filmed Frederick Duquesne (middle row, left) and other spies in an office set up for Sebold.

In August 1963, Dr. King (first row, far left) gave his "I Have a Dream" speech as part of the March on Washington.

break-ins, and mail interceptions. If FBI officials suspected someone of engaging in radical activities, they monitored that person's political interests, tapped his or her phone, and opened personal mail to collect information, even before a crime was ever committed.

Throughout the **Cold War**, whatever methods the FBI employed in its crusade against communism went unquestioned. However, doubts about its dealings with the **Mafia** were another matter. To appease the public's request that the FBI do more to investigate Mafia crimes, Hoover started the FBI's Top Hoodlum Program in 1953 to gather information on suspected mobsters around the country, but such an endeavor proved difficult. On November 14, 1957, the FBI caught a break when a New York state trooper uncovered a secret meeting of some 60 mob leaders at the Apalachin, New York, estate of crime boss Joseph Barbara Sr. The Bureau was able to renew its efforts to link such criminals through a web of conspiracies.

During the 1960s, new social movements took shape to advocate for the equality and civil rights of all Americans, regardless of race or gender. Groups spoke out against nuclear weapons testing and the Vietnam War. And many people began to question authority figures, including the FBI. In response to fears about the latest "radical" movements, the FBI expanded its secret Communist Infiltration (COMINFIL) program to include investigations of civil rights leaders such as Martin Luther King Jr. and Gloria Steinem, and organizations such as the Black Panthers and Students for a Democratic Society.

Toward the end of the decade, some officials abandoned their long-held beliefs on the importance of states' rights in favor of a federal effort to combat the urban race riots and antiwar protests. Congress passed the Omnibus Crime Control and Safe Streets Act of 1968 to put $50 million of federal funds in the hands of local law enforcement. The Racketeer Influenced and Corrupt Organization Act (RICO) of 1970 made it illegal to operate a business that was acquired, maintained, or funded through illegal activities. Many Mafia families used legitimate businesses as money-laundering fronts for gambling and

... whatever methods the FBI employed in its crusade against communism went unquestioned.

drug trafficking enterprises, and RICO finally gave the FBI grounds to arrest them.

In March 1971, the FBI was dealt a crushing blow, though. A group of Vietnam War protesters broke into an FBI field office in Media, Pennsylvania. They stole hundreds of documents that exposed the FBI's Counterintelligence Program (COINTELPRO) and the existence of Hoover's secret files on prominent Americans and members of Congress. Four years later, special committees were established to investigate the FBI's foreign and domestic activities. When its long-held, invasive practices were revealed, public confidence in the FBI plummeted. In March 1976, attorney general Edward Levi authorized the DOJ to closely supervise FBI investigations of security threats. Levi also limited preliminary investigations to no longer than 90 days and required full investigations to be supported by evidence.

To regain the trust and confidence of Congress and the American people, the FBI began to employ new technologies and procedures such as **criminal profiling**, computers, **DNA analysis**, and sting operations to combat crime in the 1980s. FBI directors Clarence Kelley and William Webster focused on breaking up Mafia families and prosecuting **white-collar** criminals. About 2,500 organized crime bosses

AGENCY INSIDER

JULIUS AND ETHEL ROSENBERG

The espionage case of Julius and Ethel Rosenberg made worldwide headlines in the early 1950s. On June 17, 1950, Julius was arrested by the FBI and accused of passing atomic secrets to the Soviet Union. Ethel was arrested two months later. The Rosenbergs vigorously proclaimed their innocence, but after a brief trial in 1951, they were sentenced to death. On June 19, 1953, the Rosenbergs became the only U.S. civilians to be executed for espionage during the Cold War.

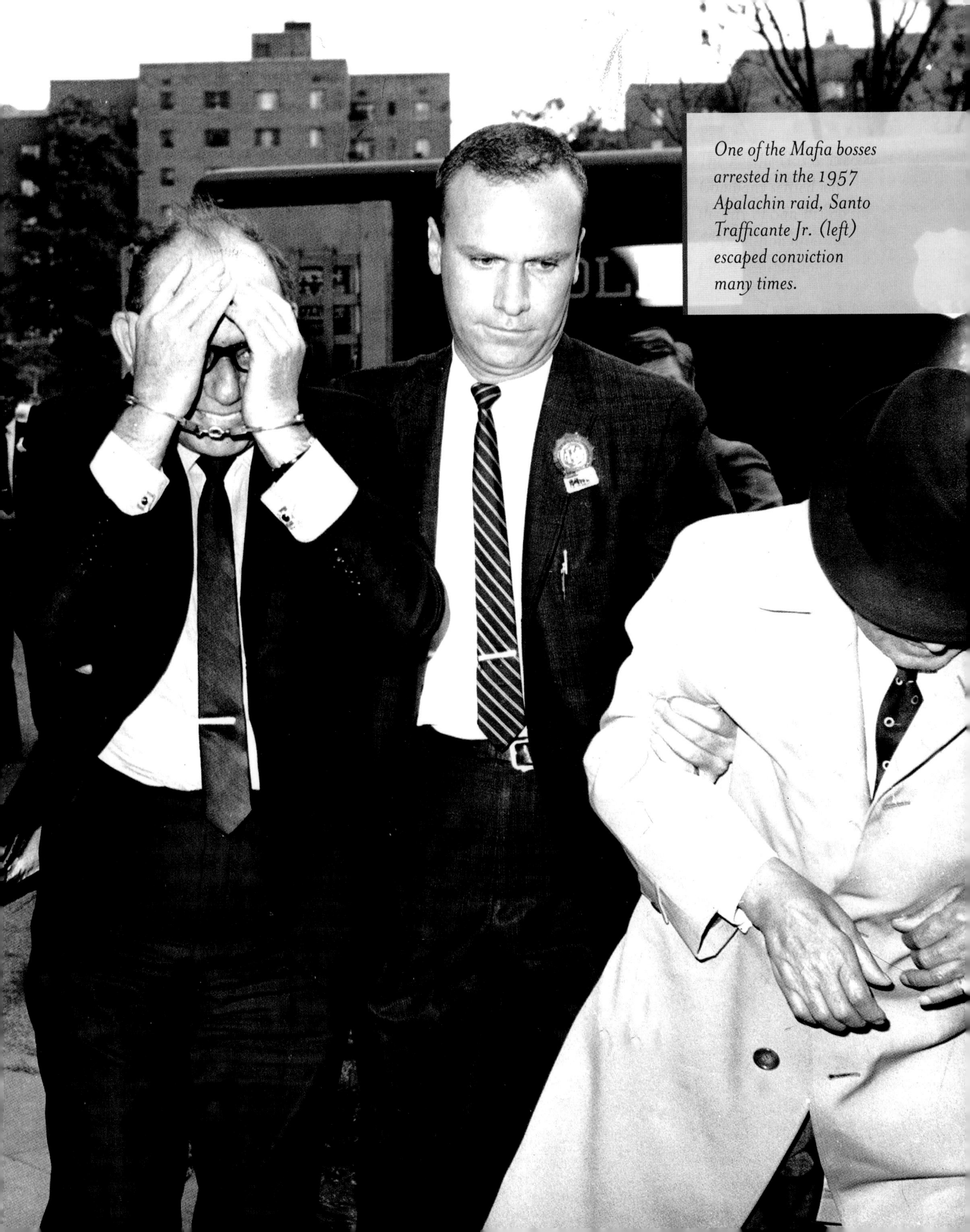

One of the Mafia bosses arrested in the 1957 Apalachin raid, Santo Trafficante Jr. (left) escaped conviction many times.

and associates were convicted between 1981 and 1985. With the collapse of the Soviet Union and end of the Cold War in 1991, the FBI again changed its focus to center on new threats of terrorism, both foreign and domestic.

On September 11, 2001, 19 militants associated with the Islamic fundamentalist group al Qaeda hijacked 4 planes, crashing 2 into New York's World Trade Center, 1 into the Pentagon, and 1 into a Pennsylvania field. The terror attacks killed nearly 3,000 people, becoming the deadliest of their kind in U.S. history. As part of the government's aggressive response, president George W. Bush authorized the USA Patriot Act of 2001, which gave the FBI access to the records of any business or individual suspected of "harboring" or "supporting" terrorists. The funding and personnel given to the FBI's Counterterrorism Division after 9/11 also greatly increased. The death of al Qaeda leader Osama bin Laden in May 2011 removed America's most wanted terrorist, but terror threats remained prominent on the FBI's radar.

Suspected Mafia families such as the Colombos flaunted their power by staging demonstrations against the FBI.

PUBLIC ENEMY NO. 1
Chicago, Illinois, U.S.A.

John Dillinger was perhaps the most infamous gang-ster of the Depression era. From September 1933 to July 1934, he and his gang killed 10 people, wounded 7, robbed banks and police arsenals, and staged 3 jail-breaks. The FBI labeled Dillinger Public Enemy No. 1. On July 22, 1934, Dillinger was shot and killed by FBI agents outside a movie theater in Chicago, Illinois, finally putting an end to his crime spree.

Stabilizing Structure

From its meager beginnings in 1908, the FBI has grown greatly both in size and significance. However, it still continues to investigate crimes and gather intelligence. The FBI has the authority to investigate more than 200 categories of federal crimes, including those occurring on American Indian reservations. It is a field-oriented organization composed of nine divisions and three offices headquartered at the J. Edgar Hoover Building in Washington, D.C. These FBI divisions and offices provide program direction and support services to 56 field offices, approximately 380 smaller offices known as resident agencies, 4 specialized field installations, and more than 60 international legal attaché offices. The legal attaché offices work with American and foreign authorities to fight organized crime, international terrorism, foreign counterintelligence, and general criminal matters in foreign countries.

FBI staff has also grown significantly throughout the past century. In 2014, the FBI employed more than 34,000 permanent positions, including special agents, intelligence

The FBI shared office space with the DOJ until its own headquarters on Pennsylvania Avenue was completed in 1975.

analysts, scientists, and other professionals. FBI funding is overseen by Congress because it comes from the federal budget. The FBI's 2013 budget totaled $8.2 billion, which provided critical support to address threats posed by terrorists, cyber attackers, and criminals.

Because the FBI is part of the DOJ, the U.S. attorney general is at the top of the chain of command. However, the attorney general does not exercise direct authority over the FBI itself— that is the job of the inspector general. Before 2002, the inspector general could investigate the FBI only with the attorney general's permission. After several scandals in 2001—including the revelation that FBI agent Robert Hanssen had been selling U.S. secrets to the Soviet Union and Russia for 15 to 22 years—Congress gave the inspector general more oversight power. The director of national intelligence oversees the FBI's intelligence activities.

The FBI is headed by a director, who is appointed by the U.S. president and confirmed by the Senate to serve a 10-year term.

The FBI is headed by a director, who is appointed by the U.S. president and confirmed by the Senate to serve a 10-year term. The director is responsible for managing the daily operations of the FBI. Assisted by a deputy director and associate director, the director ensures cases and operations are handled correctly and is in charge of assigning agents to the FBI's field offices. On September 4, 2013, James B. Comey was sworn in as the seventh director of the FBI. A native of Yonkers, New York, Comey earned his law degree from the University of Chicago Law School and then worked as an assistant U.S. attorney in southern New York and eastern Virginia. There he was known for taking on numerous organized crime and terrorism cases. As FBI director, Comey faced the challenges of preventing terrorist attacks and defusing cyber threats, all amidst budget cuts and staff reductions.

An executive assistant director manages each of the FBI's five main branches: Criminal, Cyber, Response, and Services; Human Resources; Information Technology; National Security; and Science and Technology. Each branch is split into subdivisions, with each of those headed by an assistant director. The various divisions and other offices are further broken into sub-branches led by deputy assistant directors. Within these sub-branches, there are various sections headed by section chiefs. Three of the branches report to the deputy director, while two report to the associate director.

Prior to becoming director of the FBI, James Comey served as U.S. deputy attorney general, an office of the DOJ.

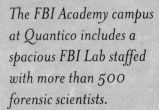

The FBI Academy campus at Quantico includes a spacious FBI Lab staffed with more than 500 forensic scientists.

Because the FBI serves as the main law enforcement and national security agency of the U.S. government, it focuses on broad, complex investigations—from organized, drug, and white-collar crimes to domestic and international terrorism and foreign counterintelligence. The FBI also works closely with other federal, state, local, and international law enforcement and intelligence agencies. But the FBI does not decide if an individual will be prosecuted. That is the work of federal prosecutors at the DOJ.

First opened in 1972, the FBI Academy is home to the Bureau's communications and computer laboratory. The academy trains new federal law enforcement officers and houses FBI units such as the Field and Police Training Unit, Firearms Training Unit, Forensic Science Research and Training Center, Technology Services Unit (TSU), and Investigative Computer Training Unit. The FBI National Academy is a program that invites leaders in law enforcement from around the world to participate in courses covering such topics as law, fitness, and leadership development.

Training to become an FBI special agent begins at the FBI Academy in Quantico, Virginia. Every agent is required to complete 20 weeks of more than 800 hours of coursework. Internet-based classes cover four major areas: academics, case exercises, firearms training, and operational skills. For the academic portion of their training, agents study such subjects as law, ethics, behavioral science, interviewing and report writing, basic and advanced investigative and intelligence techniques, interrogation, and forensic science. They learn how to set up and run investigations that deal with counterterrorism, counterintelligence, weapons of mass destruction, and other criminal activities. All agents must also pass a physical fitness, medical, and vision test before being hired. The FBI requires agents to have at least a bachelor's degree. Agents frequently seek degrees in criminal justice, law enforcement, or homeland security.

Through case exercises, the FBI tests trainees' abilities to handle on-the-job situations. Each exercise starts with a tip that challenges participants to see the case through to comple-

Every agent is required to complete 20 weeks of more than 800 hours of coursework.

tion and arrest of the subject. These simulations take place on the streets of Hogan's Alley, the mock town on the academy's campus. They feature hired actors playing criminals and terrorists. As part of the preparation for potential deadly encounters, new agents receive firearms training with a pistol, carbine, and shotgun. Agents fire approximately 5,000 rounds of ammunition during their firearms training, and all agents must demonstrate proficiency with each weapon to pass.

Trainees also receive more than 90 hours of instruction and practical exercises focused on tactics, operations planning, physical and electronic surveillance, undercover operations, and intelligence gathering. They learn defensive tactics such as handcuffing, control holds, and taking weapons away from subjects. At Hogan's Alley, trainees conduct interviews, plan and carry out an arrest, and perform surveillance. They also participate in scenarios from robberies and kidnappings to assaults on a federal officer.

The FBI was the first law enforcement agency in the world to use the Virtual Reality Tactical Training Simulator, or VirtSim. The three-dimensional simulator immerses students in a virtual 360-degree environment. Trainees kneel, crawl, jump, and run as they

AGENCY INSIDER

THE DIRECTOR

Since William Flynn's time at the helm (1919–21), the leader of the FBI has been called "Director" rather than "Chief." Flynn (pictured) was succeeded as director by William Burns, who served for only three years before J. Edgar Hoover began his long tenure in 1924. In 1976, Congress passed Public Law 94-503, part of which provided that "the term of service of the Director of the Federal Bureau of Investigation shall be ten years."

FBI Hostage Rescue and SWAT Teams are the agency's special forces and have trained at Quantico since the 1980s.

would in real-life situations. They must make decisions, cover dangerous areas, and communicate with other team members in virtual environments, such as a school, office complex, barn, airplane, and restaurant.

Other specialized functions of the FBI are located at facilities in Quantico and in Clarksburg, West Virginia. A data campus in Clarksburg stores 100 million sets of fingerprints from individuals across the U.S., along with others collected by U.S. authorities from foreign prisoners. In 2014, Congress approved funds for a new complex to be built for the FBI's Records Management Division, which processes Freedom of Information Act (FOIA) requests, near Winchester, Virginia.

The FBI Laboratory in Quantico serves as the primary lab for most DNA, biological, and forensic work conducted by the FBI. First set up by Hoover with a handful of agents, the lab's staff eventually included handwriting analysts, forensic scientists, specialists in digital imagery and computers, and **polygraphers**. Today, the lab supports the Combined DNA Index System (CODIS), collects evidence, consults on cases involving hazardous materials, processes photography, analyzes chemicals, and decrypts codes. In addition, many state, local, and international agencies make use of the services of the FBI Laboratory for free.

Invented in 1921, the polygraph's primary function has always been to determine a suspect's truthfulness in an investigation.

THE KGB
Moscow, Russia

The Committee for State Security, better known as the KGB, was formed in 1954 to protect the Soviet Union from threats and gather intelligence worldwide. The KGB often imposed censorship and internal security measures against artistic, political, and religious opposition, and spied on Soviet and foreign citizens inside the country. As a result, it bred fear both within and beyond the Soviet Union's

STREET JOURN

Y, MAY 2, 2011 - VOL. CCLVII NO. 101 | 10-YR.TREASURY ▲ 27/32, yield 3.298% · OI

STOXX 600 283.78 ▲1.25

Ne

R

ama Bin Laden, rror Mastermind, Reported Dead

CLOUDY, RAIN
High, 54. Low, 43.
▶ B10

MONDAY, MAY 2, 2011

The Seattle Times

WINNER OF EIGHT PULITZER PRIZES

75¢ $1.00 outside King, Pierce, Snohomish, Kitsap counties

Independent and locally owne
1.6 million readers weekly in

BIN LADE
KILLED

A NATION CELEB

tice has been

THE NATION'S NEWSPAPER

SPORTS SCORES INSIDE

LeBron James: Drives past Celtics' Rajon Rondo.
By Jeffrey M. Boan, AP

Celtics feel the heat
Miami leads Eastern Conference semifinal with 99-90 win. NBA, 1, 10C

Newsline
MONDAY, MAY 2, 2011

USA TODAY

A GANNETT COMPANY

Jeff Beck

Osama bin Lad
dead, Obama s

A step toward sainthood
Masses of people fill St. Peter's Square to see John Paul II's coffin as the former pope was beatified. 7A

NATO says it wasn't targeting Gadhafi; Russia slams attack
Allied forces insists the airstrike was aimed at destroying military control center, says reports about death of Gadhafi's son not confirmed. 7A

Shuttle won't launch before Mother's Day, NASA says
Rep. Gabrielle Giffords, recovering from gunshot wound to the head, will return to watch her husband take off in Endeavour, staff says. 3A.

Ask Matt: A few can avoid paying into Social S

Vide
the ce
tion at
Freedo
Bridge is
available
at www.
thenews
tribune.
com.

INSIDE
South
Sounders
and state
leaders
react to
Osama bin
Laden's
death.
See stories,
back page.

killed him in a targeted operation
By Jim Michaels
USA TODAY

WASHINGTON — Osama bin Laden, the master
mind behind the Sept. 11 terror attacks that led to
two wars, is dead, President Obama
Sunday.
"The United States h
that has killed
were b
down by
Laden's
ers 10 years
Another

Securing the Unknown

More than a decade after the 9/11 attacks, the FBI continues to struggle with redefining itself and its priorities in an age of international terrorism. Before 9/11, the FBI had focused mainly on crimes within the country that were often violent but usually related to gang activity, drug trafficking, and organized crime. After 2001, FBI agents shifted their focus to pursuing international terrorists whom they had difficulty locating and whose motives they little understood. After the 9/11 attacks, President Bush gave attorney general John Ashcroft and FBI director Robert Mueller III a new mission: to pursue international terrorists in order to prevent such an attack from recurring. That mission led to a fundamental change in the way the FBI approaches investigations today. No longer was it enough to arrest criminals after the fact—they must be stopped before plans turned into actions. Devising legal ways of obtaining the intelligence to prevent terrorist acts continues to challenge FBI officials.

By 2013, al Qaeda leader Osama bin Laden and several other heads of terrorist organizations

Osama bin Laden's death was front-page news around the U.S. and the world the day after Navy SEALs found him.

had been killed. Al Qaeda's last successful attack in the West was in the United Kingdom in 2005. However, terrorist operatives were responsible for several attempted attacks throughout the past 10 years in the U.S., Norway, Denmark, the United Kingdom, Germany, and Pakistan. Even though these terror organizations lost members and became more loosely organized, they remained a significant global threat to safety. Apart from counterintelligence operations, the FBI also concentrates its efforts on international crime networks such as the Sicilian Mafia, Russian organized crime, and international drug cartels.

When president Barack Obama began his second term in 2013, he pledged to refocus the nation's intelligence resources on addressing other international issues such as cyber security. While new technologies have improved global communication, they have also given criminals and terrorists new opportunities to steal American property and compromise national security. People are susceptible to various forms of fraud on a daily basis, from **phishing** e-mails to malware that turns their computers into spam producers to methods of

identity theft. Through the end of 2013, foreign agents were reported to have stolen more than $1 trillion of American intellectual property. Unlike other types of property, intellectual property has value but is not an actual product that can be seen or touched. (An organization's accounting department usually sets a value on intellectual property for financial reports, tax reports, or other negotiations, though.) The U.S. government and the military face constant threats from cyber hackers trying to gain access to this critical information.

In the early 1990s, the FBI attempted to put in place methods of stopping cyber criminals in their tracks. In 1994, president Bill Clinton signed the Communications Assistance for Law Enforcement Act (CALEA) into law. CALEA allowed the FBI to conduct electronic surveillance on American citizens with the assistance of telecommunications companies—as long as it had a court order. Nearly 20 years later, the FBI lobbied for the passage of CALEA II, which would extend the original law to Internet services such as Google and Facebook. Under CALEA II, search engines and other online services would be required to allow

> *The U.S. government and the military face constant threats from cyber hackers trying to gain access ...*

Facebook tracks and reports on the number of requests it receives from the government for its users' information.

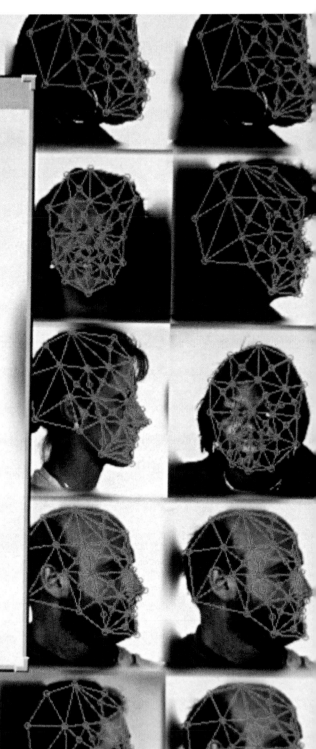

00052pr001.931230.tiff

Three-dimensional facial recognition uses data about the shape and features of a face to help identify people.

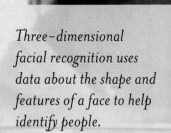

the FBI access to their customers' personal accounts, such as e-mail or online conversations—or pay a fine.

Through communications tools such as e-mail, social media, and instant messaging, people's activities can be traced more easily than ever before. Many people remain skeptical of allowing the FBI such broad monitoring authority, fearing that it would infringe on their right to privacy. In the future, Americans will have to decide how much of a digital trail they are comfortable leaving. Are the threats posed by cyber hackers and terrorists significant enough to warrant the FBI's having unrestricted access to individuals' personal data?

In its efforts to combat cyber crime, the FBI is using the new electronic technology to gather unprecedented amounts of electronic and **biometric** data about U.S. citizens. It is building large biometrics databases such as Next Generation Identification (NGI). NGI is an expansion of the FBI's fingerprint database to include palm prints, iris scans, and facial recognition. Critics of NGI have accused the FBI of

lumping together evidence gained from ordinary civilians with that from criminals. They claim that the FBI does not take enough care to keep fingerprints and other personal data obtained through governmental job applications separate from criminal data.

Between 1995 and 2013, an uptick in FBI criminal pursuit corresponded with a decrease in violent crime rates across the U.S. Continuing such success will be a challenge as the agency faces a shrinking budget and depleted staff, though. In 2013, the federal government began a series of annual budget cuts—which were to take place every year for the next eight—to save itself more than $1 trillion. As a result, in 2013 the FBI had to subtract $700 million from its yearly budget and lay off 3,000 employees. This forced FBI officials to assign fewer agents to units such as violent crime so that they could keep enough people on hand for counterterrorism operations. The agency did not hire any new agents or open new intelligence investigations in 2013, and some criminal cases had to be closed before being solved. Gas rationing also forced

In the future, Americans will have to decide how much of a digital trail they are comfortable leaving.

agents around the country to limit vehicle use, which sacrificed some surveillance work. Those conditions could prompt veteran agents to leave the FBI for higher-paying jobs in other types of law enforcement. Budget cuts could also limit the director's ability to keep the FBI's computer systems up to date, a critical part in thwarting terrorist and cyber attacks. As of 2014, though, the jobs outlook improved, and the FBI began hiring again.

Another controversial issue surrounding the FBI is its use of drones as surveillance tools. A drone is an unmanned aircraft. A computer controls its flight from a remote location. Drones are often less expensive to operate and can fly closer to structures and through some areas otherwise hidden from view more safely than manned aircraft. Drones are often used by the military to scout out places or fire missiles. However, between 2004 and 2013, the FBI spent more than $3 million to operate a fleet of small drone aircraft in domestic investigations, with almost no public knowledge. Surveillance drones have proven useful to the FBI in situations when the lives of agents were at risk. Cameras and sensors mounted on drones can track movement in the dark and detect heat signatures of people

AGENCY INSIDER

TYLENOL PANIC

In 1982, in one of the first cases of terrorism in the U.S., a string of deaths in the Chicago, Illinois, area was attributed to Tylenol laced with a highly toxic substance called potassium cyanide. The first victim was a 12-year-old girl whose parents gave her a painkiller for a cold. Six deaths followed in the next month. The FBI concluded that someone was likely tampering with the drug on store shelves, which set off a nationwide panic. Despite a lengthy investigation, no one was ever charged with the crime.

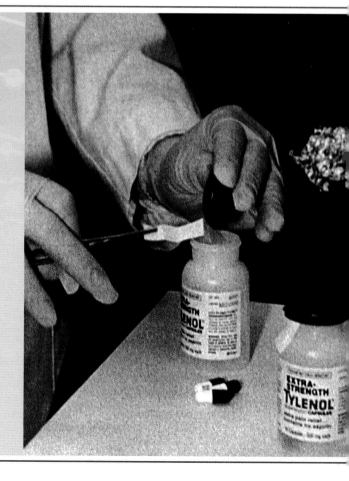

Camera–equipped quad–copters (aircraft with four rotors) represent an increasingly popular drone technology.

hiding on the ground. Drones can give agents aerial views of an active crime scene without putting a pilot in danger of being shot down. Once people found out the FBI had been using drones, though, some questioned whether such monitoring could be used improperly. In 2014, the FBI was faced with the challenges of writing new guidelines to address such concerns and of curbing improper surveillance by law enforcement drones.

Throughout the more than 100 years of the FBI's existence, the world has transformed itself from one of separate individuals acting at a slower, more independent pace to a global network linked by rapid communications technology. At the same time, the FBI's role has evolved from a pursuer of gangster bank robbers to a tracker of cyber security and terrorist threats. Along with greater responsibilities have come controversies, but the FBI has weathered them all, poised to take on the future with "Fidelity, Bravery, and Integrity."

Improvised Explosive Devices (IEDs) are sent to the FBI's Terrorist Explosive Device Analytical Center to be examined.

OKBOMB
Oklahoma City, Oklahoma, U.S.A.

On April 19, 1995, a truck-bomb exploded outside the Alfred P. Murrah Federal Building in Oklahoma City, Oklahoma, killing 168 people and injuring hundreds more. Later that day, anti-government militant Timothy McVeigh was arrested. During the FBI's investigation ("OKBOMB"), agents conducted more than 20,000 interviews and collected nearly a billion pieces of evidence, linking McVeigh and his accomplice, Terry Nichols, to the attack. McVeigh was executed in 2001, and Nichols was sentenced to life in prison.

GLOSSARY

anarchists people who rebel against any authority or ruling power

antitrust laws that protect against unfair business practices that limit competition or control prices

biometric describing the use of unique physical or behavioral characteristics (such as fingerprint or voice patterns) to verify someone's personal identity

Cold War a period of rivalry after World War II between the communist Soviet Union and the democratic United States

communist having to do with belief in a governmental system in which all property is owned by the community as a whole

corrupt guilty of dishonest practices, such as bribery

criminal profiling the act of developing a psychological description of a criminal based on how the crime scene looks, in order to help authorities identify the criminal

deport to force a foreign-born person to leave a country and return to his or her native country

DNA analysis a technique used by forensic scientists to analyze a small amount of a person's genetic material (such as blood or cells) in order to identify that individual

gangsters members of a group of violent criminals

Mafia an organized crime group that primarily uses violent intimidation to manipulate local economic activity

phishing obtaining financial information from an online account holder by posing as a legitimate company

polygraphers operators of a machine that measures a person's involuntary bodily activities such blood pressure, temperature, and pulse rate to determine if that person is telling the truth

radical advocating fundamental political, economic, and social reforms, often by extreme methods

socialist having to do with belief in the social organization of community-run production, distribution, and exchange of goods

statute of limitations a type of federal or state law that restricts the time within which legal proceedings may be brought

stock market a system for buying and selling stocks, or ownership shares in a company

union an organization made up of workers in a particular industry to promote worker rights

white-collar describing office and professional workers whose jobs generally do not involve blue-collar manual labor or wearing a uniform or work clothes

SELECTED BIBLIOGRAPHY

Holden, Henry M. *FBI 100 Years: An Unofficial History*. Minneapolis: Zenith Press, 2008.

Jeffreys-Jones, Rhodri. *The FBI: A History*. New Haven: Yale University Press, 2008.

Kessler, Ronald. *The Bureau: The Secret History of the FBI*. New York: St. Martin's Press, 2003.

Kessler, Ronald. *The Secrets of the FBI*. New York: Crown, 2011.

Theoharis, Athan G. *The FBI & American Democracy: A Brief Critical History*. Lawrence: University Press of Kansas, 2004.

United States Department of Justice. The FBI: Federal Bureau of Investigation. http://www.fbi.gov/.

Weiner, Tim. *Enemies: A History of the FBI*. New York: Random House, 2012.

WEBSITES

FBI Kids Page
http://www.fbi.gov/fun-games/kids/kids
Learn about how the FBI investigates crimes, and participate in your own FBI agent adventure and challenge.

Kids Ahead: Crime Scene Investigation Activities
http://kidsahead.com/subjects/10-crime-scene-investigation/activities
Help investigate criminal cases and crash scenes, and discover your unique fingerprint!

Note: Every effort has been made to ensure that the websites listed above are suitable for children, that they have educational value, and that they contain no inappropriate material. However, because of the nature of the Internet, it is impossible to guarantee that these sites will remain active indefinitely or that their contents will not be altered.

INDEX

al Qaeda 24, 37, 38

attorneys general 8, 11, 12, 22, 28, 37
   Ashcroft, John 37
   Bonaparte, Charles 8
   Levi, Edward 22
   Palmer, A. Mitchell 12
   Wickersham, George 8, 11

bin Laden, Osama 24, 37

Bureau of Investigation (BOI) 8, 11, 12, 14, 17, 18, 32
   chief/director 8, 11, 14, 32
   Identification Division 14
   overseeing of the GID 11, 12
   training school 14
   types of cases 11, 17, 18

Bush, George W. 24, 37

Clarksburg, West Virginia 34

Clinton, Bill 38

Cold War 21, 22, 24, 35
   KGB 35

communism 11, 12, 18, 21
   and Communist Infiltration Program 21

databases 14, 34, 41
   fingerprint 14, 34
   Next Generation Identification 41

Department of Justice (DOJ) 7, 8, 11, 12, 18, 22, 28, 31
   early federal investigations 7, 8
   federal prosecutors 31
   General Intelligence Division (GID) 11, 12
   U.S. inspector general 28

famous cases 15, 17, 18, 42, 45
   Brink's Robbery 15
   Duquesne Spy Ring 18
   Lindbergh Baby 17
   Oklahoma City bombing 45
   Tylenol Panic 42

FBI Academy 31–32, 34
   National Academy program 31
   special agent training 31–32
   units of 31
   Virtual Reality Tactical Training Simulator 32, 34

FBI directors 8, 12, 14, 18, 22, 28, 32, 34, 37, 42
   Burns, William 32
   Comey, James B. 28
   Finch, Stanley W. 8
   Flynn, William 32
   Hoover, J. Edgar 12, 14, 18, 22, 32, 34

Kelley, Clarence 22
   Mueller, Robert III 37
   Webster, William 22

FBI Laboratory 14, 34
   and Combined DNA Index System 34
   origins as Criminology Laboratory 14
   services 34

FBI organization 27–28, 32, 41, 42
   Congressional funding 28, 41
   field installations 27
   field offices 27, 28
   international legal attaché offices 27
   resident agencies 27
   staff 27–28, 41

Goldman, Emma 12

Hanssen, Robert 28

Hauptmann, Bruno Richard 18

investigatory authority 4, 8, 11, 17, 18, 21, 22, 24, 25, 27,
      28, 31, 37, 38, 41, 44
   counterintelligence 18, 21, 22, 27, 31, 38
   counterterrorism 24, 27, 28, 31, 37, 41, 44
   cyber attacks 28, 38, 41, 44
   drug trafficking 31, 37, 38
   espionage 18, 22
   expanded by laws 11, 18, 21, 22, 24, 38
   gang activity 37
   gangster crime 17, 25
   in law enforcement 4, 8, 17, 27, 31, 44
   monitoring of communications 38, 41
   in national security 4, 18, 22, 31, 38, 44
   organized crime 21, 22, 27, 28, 31, 37, 38
   white-collar crime 22, 31

J. Edgar Hoover Building 27

McVeigh, Timothy 45

Nichols, Terry 45

Obama, Barack 38

Palmer Raids 12

Putin, Vladimir 35

Quantico, Virginia 31, 34

Red Scare 11

Roosevelt, Theodore 4, 8

Rosenberg, Julius and Ethel 22

September 11 attacks 24, 37

surveillance drones 42, 44

World War I 11

World War II 18